Practical
Party Food

p^3

This is a P³ Book
First published in 2003

P³
Queen Street House
4 Queen Street
Bath BA1 1HE, UK

ISBN: 1-40540-923–1

Printed in China

NOTE

This book uses metric and imperial measurements. Follow the same units
of measurement throughout; do not mix metric and imperial.
All spoon measurements are level: teaspoons are assumed to be 5 ml, and
tablespoons are assumed to be 15 ml. Unless otherwise stated,
milk is assumed to be full fat, eggs and individual vegetables such as potatoes
are medium, and pepper is freshly ground black pepper.

The nutritional information provided for each recipe is per serving or per person.
Optional ingredients, variations, or serving suggestions have
not been included in the calculations. The times given for each recipe are an approximate
guide only because the preparation times may differ according to the techniques used by
different people and the cooking times may vary as a result of the type of oven used.

Recipes using raw or very lightly cooked eggs should be
avoided by children, the elderly, pregnant women, convalescents,
and anyone suffering from an illness.

Contents

Introduction

Whether a long-planned celebration or an impromptu gathering, a party is always a uniquely special occasion. It may also be hard work, stressful, expensive and exhausting for the host – with no guarantee of success. Yet it should be as much fun to throw a party as it is to attend one. Only you can decide whether your guests will get on with each other or if you can afford to serve champagne, but this book can at least take away any worries about what snacks to serve.

This book features a wide range of vegetarian recipes as well as fish and meat recipes, so that you can be sure to please everyone. Most of these are finger foods, minimizing the amount of preparation and clearing up you will need to do, although there are a few dishes that require a fork to eat them. The emphasis throughout is on tasty treats that are easy to prepare. After all, we all want our guests to enjoy the food but we do not want to spend so much time in the kitchen that we are too tired to enjoy ourselves.

Dips and pâtés offer a fabulous collection of international recipes for easy entertaining, and this book features a spectacular selection, such as Black Olive Pâté (see page 6) and Authentic Guacamole (see page 13). All of these can be made in advance and can be laid out in a tempting array with a selection of different breads. Individual recipes also provide specific serving suggestions to help you choose other accompaniments. This book is an excellent source of reference for the

main constituents of your buffet table, and provides a wide choice of recipes for savoury nibbles and snacks, from delicious nachos and tartlets, to Indian treats and Italian mini pizzas. There are recipes for traditional favourites, such as tiny cheese balls (see Toasted Nibbles on page 22) and Mini Cheese & Onion Tarts (see page 30). For party foods with more international flavours, why not try the Taramasalata with Pittas (see page 17), Samosas (see page 21), or the Provençal Tart (see page 32)? While all these snacks are delicious cold, some can also be served warm or hot if you prefer. Hot nibbles are always a special treat, but it is easy to be over-ambitious. Most of the recipes in this book are either very speedy or can be prepared in advance and popped in the oven or grilled when your guests have arrived.

Whatever kind of party you are planning, from a simple family gathering to a crowded New Year celebration, in this book you will find delicious bites and morsels, and mouthwatering canapés and snacks for every occasion.

Party basics

Do not forget that there are plenty of ready-made nibbles that you can buy to increase the variety of your party snacks. For example, if you are short of time, you can buy plain and flavoured breadsticks. However, if you have more time, why not try making your own? Your guests will find the Sesame Breadsticks (see page 18) irresistible. Corn chips, tortilla chips, and plain potato crisps are ideal for

dunking into home-made dips or just nibbling on their own. Peanuts are party favourites, but you can also include cashew nuts, almonds and pistachio nuts. A selection of cheeses and a basket of crackers or crusty bread are also easy to produce and always popular.

If you are already planning to prepare a range of flavoursome foods, you can supplement them with some simpler snacks, such as grilled chicken drumsticks, sausages on sticks, and squares of toast with ready-made toppings, such as lumpfish roe, sliced hard-boiled eggs, smoked salmon, slices of salami, and soft cheese and chives. Try garnishing them with herb sprigs, sliced stuffed olives, pearl onions or tiny gherkins. Sandwiches are usually best avoided because they quickly dry out. However, you may well be tempted by the mozzarella sandwiches in this book (see Mozzarella Snack on page 26). These delicious sandwiches are deep-fried, and should be served while still hot.

If you do not mind providing cutlery as well as plates, you can also serve a selection of salads. Most supermarkets sell a wide selection of mixed leaf and vegetable salads that are ideal. Pasta and rice salads with a colourful mixture of drained canned sweetcorn, red and yellow pepper strips, tomato wedges, cooked frozen peas, and strips of ham are easily made and can be dressed with a vinaigrette dressing or mayonnaise, or try serving them with Aïoli (see page 16).

Crudités

Raw and blanched vegetables are perfect for serving with most dips and look very tempting on a large serving platter. Deseed and slice red, yellow or orange peppers lengthways. Blanch baby corn and trimmed, thin asparagus in lightly salted boiling water. Your crudités can include whole cherry tomatoes, small button mushrooms and trimmed radishes, perhaps with a few small leaves attached. Trim and separate the leaves of red and white chicory or the hearts of lettuces. Cut raw cauliflower into small florets and slice carrots, celery and cucumber into sticks.

Vegetable crisps

Home-made vegetable crisps make a delicious alternative to ordinary potato crisps. You can, of course, use potatoes, but you might also like to try parsnips, carrots or sweet potatoes. Peel the vegetables and slice very thinly using a mandoline or swivel-bladed vegetable peeler. Heat sunflower or ground nut oil in a deep-fryer or large saucepan to 180–190°C/350–375°F, or until a cube of day-old bread browns in 30 seconds. Add the vegetable slices to the oil and cook until golden. Drain on kitchen paper and sprinkle with sea salt, paprika or cayenne pepper. Store in an airtight container when cold.

KEY	
	Simplicity level 1–3 (1 easiest, 3 slightly harder)
	Preparation time
	Cooking time

Black Olive Pâté

This pâté is delicious served as a party snack on small circles of fried bread. It can also be served as a starter on pieces of toasted bread.

NUTRITIONAL INFORMATION

Calories	149	Sugars	.........1g
Protein	.........2g	Fat	..........14g
Carbohydrate	....4g	Saturates	.......6g

 5 mins   5 mins

SERVES 4

I N G R E D I E N T S

225 g/8 oz stoned juicy black olives

1 garlic clove, crushed

finely grated rind of 1 lemon

4 tbsp lemon juice

25 g/1 oz fresh breadcrumbs

60 g/2¼ oz full-fat cream cheese

salt and pepper

lemon wedges, to garnish

TO SERVE

thick slices of bread

mixture of olive oil and butter

1 Coarsely chop the olives and mix with the garlic, lemon rind and juice, breadcrumbs and cream cheese. Pound the mixture until smooth, or place in a food processor and work until fully blended. Season to taste with salt and freshly ground black pepper.

2 Store the pâté in a screw-top jar and chill for several hours before using – this allows the flavours to develop.

3 For a delicious cocktail snack, use a biscuit cutter to cut out small circles from a thickly sliced loaf.

4 Cook the bread circles in a mixture of olive oil and butter until they are a light golden-brown colour. Drain well on kitchen paper.

5 Top each circle with a little of the pâté, garnish with lemon wedges, and serve immediately. This pâté will keep chilled in an airtight jar for up to 2 weeks.

Cheese, Garlic & Herb Pâté

This wonderful cream cheese pâté is fragrant with the aroma of fresh herbs and garlic. Serve with triangles of Melba toast for a perfect party food.

NUTRITIONAL INFORMATION

Calories 392	Sugars 1g	
Protein 17g	Fat 28g	
Carbohydrate ...18g	Saturates 18g	

 20 mins   10 mins

SERVES 4

I N G R E D I E N T S

1 tbsp butter

1 garlic clove, crushed

3 spring onions, finely chopped

125 g/4½ oz full-fat cream cheese

2 tbsp chopped mixed herbs, such as parsley, chives, marjoram, oregano and basil

175 g/6 oz mature Cheddar cheese, finely grated

4–6 slices of white bread from a medium-cut sliced loaf

mixed salad leaves and cherry tomatoes, to serve

T O   G A R N I S H

ground paprika

sprigs of fresh herbs

3 Add the Cheddar cheese and work the mixture together to form a stiff paste. Cover and chill until ready to serve.

4 To make the Melba toast, toast the slices of bread on both sides, and then cut off the crusts. Using a sharp bread knife, cut through the slices horizontally to make very thin slices. Cut into triangles and then lightly toast the untoasted sides until golden.

5 Arrange the mixed salad leaves on 4 serving plates with the cherry tomatoes. Pile the cheese pâté on top and sprinkle with a little paprika. Garnish with sprigs of fresh herbs and serve with the Melba toast.

1 Melt the butter in a small frying pan and gently sauté the garlic and spring onions together for 3–4 minutes until soft. Leave them to cool.

2 Beat the cream cheese in a large mixing bowl until smooth, then add the garlic and spring onions. Stir in the chopped mixed herbs, mixing well.

Tuna & Anchovy Pâté

An excellent tangy combination, which can be used for a sandwich filling or as a dip. The pâté will keep well in the refrigerator for up to a week.

NUTRITIONAL INFORMATION	
Calories 183	Sugars 3g
Protein 25g	Fat 6g
Carbohydrate 9g	Saturates 2g

🥘 1¼ hrs   🕐 25 mins

SERVES 6

INGREDIENTS

50 g/1¾ oz canned anchovy fillets, drained

400 g/14 oz canned tuna in brine, drained

175 g/6 oz low-fat cottage cheese

125 g/4½ oz skimmed milk soft cheese

1 tbsp horseradish relish

½ tsp grated orange rind

white pepper

4 thick slices wholemeal bread, to serve

TO GARNISH

orange slices

sprigs of fresh dill

1 Separate the anchovy fillets and pat well with kitchen paper to remove all traces of oil.

2 Put the anchovies, tuna, cheeses, horseradish relish and orange rind in a blender or food processor. Season with white pepper and process for a few seconds until smooth. Alternatively, finely chop the anchovy fillets and flake the tuna, then beat together with the other ingredients – this will make a more textured pâté.

3 Transfer to a mixing bowl, cover, and chill for 1 hour.

4 Place the wholemeal bread slices under a preheated medium grill and toast for 2–3 minutes on each side until lightly browned.

5 Using a serrated knife, slice off the crusts and slide the knife between the toasted edges of the bread.

6 Stamp out circles using a 5-cm/2-inch biscuit cutter and place on a baking sheet. Alternatively, cut each piece of toast in half diagonally. Bake the toasted circles in a preheated oven, 150°C/300°F/Gas Mark 2, for 15–20 minutes until curled and dry.

7 Spoon the pâté on to serving plates and then garnish with orange slices and sprigs of fresh dill. Serve with the freshly baked croûtons.

Parsley, Chicken & Ham Pâté

Pâté is easy to make at home, and this combination of lean chicken and ham mixed with herbs is especially straightforward.

NUTRITIONAL INFORMATION

Calories	119	Sugars	.........2g
Protein	........20g	Fat	..........3g
Carbohydrate	....2g	Saturates	......1g

 40 mins   0 mins

SERVES 4

INGREDIENTS

225 g/8 oz skinless, boneless, lean chicken, cooked

100 g/3½ oz lean ham

small bunch of fresh parsley

1 tsp grated lime zest, plus extra to garnish

2 tbsp lime juice

1 garlic clove, peeled

125 g/4½ oz low-fat natural fromage frais

salt and pepper

TO SERVE

lime wedges

crispbread or Melba toast

salad leaves

1 Coarsely dice the chicken. Trim off and discard any fat from the ham and dice the meat. Place the chicken and ham in a blender or food processor.

2 Add the parsley, lime zest and juice, and garlic and process until finely minced. Alternatively, finely chop the chicken, ham, parsley and garlic and place in a bowl. Gently stir in the lime zest and lime juice.

3 Transfer the mixture to a bowl and stir in the fromage frais. Season with salt and pepper to taste, cover with clingfilm, and chill in the refrigerator for about 30 minutes.

4 Spoon the pâté into individual serving dishes and garnish with extra grated lime zest. Serve the pâté with lime wedges, crispbread or Melba toast, and fresh salad leaves.

VARIATION

This pâté can be made successfully with other kinds of minced, lean, cooked meat, such as turkey, beef, and pork. Alternatively, replace the meat with peeled prawns and/or white crab meat, or with canned tuna in brine, drained.

Hummus & Garlic Toasts

Hummus is a real favourite, spread on these garlic toasts for a delicious party food or as part of a nutritious light lunch.

NUTRITIONAL INFORMATION

Calories	731	Sugars	.........2g
Protein	........22g	Fat	..........55g
Carbohydrate	...39g	Saturates	.......8g

 10–15 mins 5 mins

SERVES 4

I N G R E D I E N T S

H U M M U S

400 g/14 oz canned chickpeas

juice of 1 large lemon

6 tbsp tahini

2 tbsp olive oil

2 garlic cloves, finely chopped

salt and pepper

G A R L I C   T O A S T S

1 ciabatta loaf, sliced

2 garlic cloves, finely chopped

1 tbsp chopped fresh coriander

4 tbsp olive oil

T O   G A R N I S H

chopped fresh coriander

stoned black olives

1 To make the hummus, drain the chickpeas (reserve the liquid). Blend in a food processor, gradually adding the lemon juice and reserved liquid. Blend well after each addition until smooth.

2 Stir in the tahini and all but 1 teaspoon of the olive oil. Add the garlic, season, and blend until smooth.

3 Spoon the hummus into a serving dish. Drizzle the remaining olive oil over the top, and garnish with chopped coriander and stoned black olives. Chill in the refrigerator while preparing the toasts.

4 To make the toasts, lay the ciabatta slices on a grill rack in a single layer.

5 Mix the garlic, coriander and olive oil together and drizzle over the bread slices. Cook the slices under a hot grill for 2–3 minutes, turning once, until golden brown. Serve hot with the hummus.

Buttered Nut & Lentil Dip

This unusual and tasty dip is very easy to make. Almonds and spices add a distinctive Middle Eastern accent.

NUTRITIONAL INFORMATION

Calories	395	Sugars	.........4g
Protein	........12g	Fat	..........31g
Carbohydrate	...18g	Saturates	......10g

🍲 5–10 mins   ⏱ 40 mins

SERVES 4

I N G R E D I E N T S

4 tbsp butter

1 small onion, chopped

90 g/3¼ oz red lentils

300 ml/10 fl oz vegetable stock

60 g/2¼ oz blanched almonds

60 g/2¼ oz pine kernels

½ tsp ground coriander

½ tsp ground cumin

½ tsp grated root ginger

1 tsp chopped fresh coriander

salt and pepper

sprigs of fresh coriander, to garnish

TO SERVE

fresh vegetable crudités

breadsticks

1 Melt half the butter in a saucepan, add the onion, and sauté over a medium heat, stirring frequently, until it is golden brown in colour.

2 Add the lentils and vegetable stock. Bring to the boil, then lower the heat and simmer gently, uncovered, for about 25–30 minutes until the lentils are tender. Drain well.

3 Melt the remaining butter in a small frying pan. Add the almonds and pine kernels and cook them over a low heat, stirring frequently, until golden brown. Remove the pan from the heat.

4 Put the lentils, almonds and pine kernels in a food processor or blender, together with any butter remaining in the frying pan. Add the ground coriander, cumin, grated fresh ginger and chopped coriander. Process for about 15–20 seconds until the mixture is smooth. Alternatively, press the lentils through a sieve with the back of a wooden spoon to purée them and then mix with the finely chopped nuts, spices and herbs.

5 Season the dip with salt and pepper and garnish with sprigs of fresh coriander. Serve with fresh vegetable crudités and breadsticks.

VARIATION

Green or brown lentils can be used, but they will take longer to cook than red lentils. If you prefer, substitute peanuts for the almonds. Ground ginger can be used instead of fresh – substitute ½ teaspoon and add it with the other spices.

Tsatziki

This creamy Greek dip is simple to make and very refreshing on a hot day. It is particularly good for parties.

NUTRITIONAL INFORMATION	
Calories 75	Sugars 2g
Protein 4g	Fat 6g
Carbohydrate 2g	Saturates 3g

🥄 🥄

🥟 3½ hrs   🕐 3–5 mins

SERVES 12

I N G R E D I E N T S

2 large cucumbers

600 ml/1 pint thick natural yogurt

3 garlic cloves, crushed

1 tbsp finely chopped fresh dill

1 tbsp extra-virgin olive oil

salt and pepper

TO GARNISH

1 tbsp sesame seeds

cayenne pepper

sprigs of fresh dill (optional)

1 Using the coarse side of a grater, grate the cucumbers into a bowl lined with an absorbent, perforated kitchen cloth. Pull up the corners of the cloth to make a tight bundle and squeeze very hard to extract all the moisture (see Cook's Tip).

2 Put the cucumbers in a bowl and stir in the yogurt, garlic, dill and olive oil. Season with salt and pepper to taste. Cover with clingfilm and chill for at least 3 hours to allow the flavours to blend.

3 When ready to serve, remove the dip from the refrigerator and stir. Taste and adjust the seasoning if necessary.

4 Put the sesame seeds in a small, ungreased frying pan and dry-fry them over a medium heat until they turn golden and start to give off their aroma. Immediately pour them out of the pan on to the tsatziki – they will sizzle.

5 Sprinkle some cayenne pepper on to a plate. Lightly dip the tip of a dry pastry brush into the cayenne, then tap a light sprinkling of cayenne all over the tsatziki. Garnish with sprigs of fresh dill, if using, and serve. (Ungarnished tsatziki will keep for up to 3 days in the refrigerator.)

COOK'S TIP
It is essential to squeeze all the moisture out of the cucumbers in step 1, or the dip will be unpleasantly watery and will separate.

Authentic Guacamole

Guacamole is at its best when freshly made, with enough texture to really taste the avocado. Serve with vegetable sticks or tortilla chips.

NUTRITIONAL INFORMATION

Calories 212   Sugars 1g
Protein . . . . .2g   Fat 21g
Carbohydrate . . . .3g   Saturates 4g

 15 mins   0 mins

SERVES 4

I N G R E D I E N T S

1 ripe tomato

2 limes

2–3 ripe, small-to-medium avocados, or
 1–2 large ones

¼–½ onion, finely chopped

pinch of ground cumin

pinch of mild chilli powder

½–1 fresh green chilli, such as jalapeño or
 serrano, deseeded and finely chopped

1 tbsp finely chopped fresh coriander
 leaves, plus extra for garnishing

salt (optional)

tortilla chips or vegetable sticks,
 to serve (optional)

1 Put the tomato in a heatproof bowl, cover with boiling water, and leave to stand for 30 seconds. Drain and plunge into cold water. Peel off the skin. Cut the tomato in half, deseed, and chop the flesh.

2 Squeeze the juice from the limes into a small bowl. Cut 1 avocado in half around the stone. Twist the 2 halves apart in opposite directions, then remove the stone with a knife. Carefully peel off the skin, dice the flesh, and toss in the bowl of lime juice to prevent the flesh discolouring. Repeat with the remaining avocados. Mash the avocado flesh fairly coarsely with a fork.

3 Add the onion, tomato, cumin, chilli powder, fresh chilli and fresh coriander to the avocados. If using as a dip for tortilla chips, do not add salt. If using as a dip for vegetable sticks, add salt to taste.

4 To serve the guacamole, transfer to a serving dish, garnish with finely chopped fresh coriander, and serve with tortilla chips or vegetable sticks.

VARIATION

Try spooning guacamole into soups, especially chicken or seafood, or spreading it into sandwiches on thick crusty rolls. Spoon guacamole over refried beans and melted cheese, then eat it with salsa and crisp tortilla chips.

Mint & Cannellini Bean Dip

This dip is ideal for pre-dinner drinks or for handing around at a party.
The cannellini beans require soaking overnight, so prepare in advance.

NUTRITIONAL INFORMATION

Calories 208	Sugars 1g
Protein 10g	Fat 12g
Carbohydrate ...16g	Saturates 2g

 40 mins 30 mins

SERVES 6

I N G R E D I E N T S

175 g/6 oz dried cannellini beans

1 small garlic clove, crushed

1 bunch of spring onions, coarsely chopped

handful of fresh mint leaves

2 tbsp tahini

2 tbsp olive oil

1 tsp ground cumin

1 tsp ground coriander

lemon juice

salt and pepper

sprigs of fresh mint, to garnish

T O   S E R V E

fresh vegetable crudités, such as
  cauliflower florets, carrots, cucumber,
  radishes and peppers

1 Put the cannellini beans in a bowl and then add sufficient cold water to cover. Set them aside to soak for at least 4 hours or overnight.

2 Rinse and drain the beans, put them into a large saucepan, and cover them with cold water. Bring to the boil, then boil rapidly for 10 minutes. Lower the heat, cover, and simmer until tender.

3 Drain the beans thoroughly and transfer them to a bowl or food processor. Add the garlic, spring onions, mint, tahini and olive oil. Process the mixture for about 15 seconds or mash well by hand until smooth.

4 Scrape the mixture into a bowl, if necessary, then stir in the cumin, coriander and lemon juice. Season to taste

with salt and pepper. Mix thoroughly, cover with clingfilm, and set aside in a cool place, but not the refrigerator, for 30 minutes to let the flavours develop.

5 Spoon the dip into individual serving bowls and garnish with sprigs of fresh mint. Place the bowls on plates and surround them with vegetable crudités. Serve at room temperature.

Heavenly Garlic Dip

Anyone who loves garlic will adore this dip – it is very potent! Serve it at a barbecue party and dip raw vegetables or chunks of French bread into it.

NUTRITIONAL INFORMATION

Calories ....344 Sugars 2g
Protein ....6g Fat 34g
Carbohydrate ....3g Saturates 5g

 15 mins   20 mins

SERVES 4

INGREDIENTS

2 bulbs of garlic

6 tbsp olive oil

1 small onion, finely chopped

2 tbsp lemon juice

3 tbsp tahini

2 tbsp chopped fresh parsley

salt and pepper

sprigs of fresh parsley, to garnish

fresh vegetable crudités, French bread, or warmed pitta breads, to serve

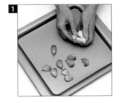

1 Separate the bulbs of garlic into individual cloves. Place them on a baking sheet and roast in a preheated oven, 200°C/400°F/Gas Mark 6, for 8–10 minutes. Set them aside to cool for a few minutes.

2 When they are cool enough to handle, peel the garlic cloves and then chop them finely.

3 Heat the olive oil in a saucepan or frying pan and add the garlic and onion. Sauté over a low heat, stirring occasionally, for 8–10 minutes until soft. Remove the pan from the heat.

4 Mix in the lemon juice, tahini, and parsley. Season to taste with salt and pepper. Transfer the dip to a small heatproof bowl and keep warm at one side of the barbecue.

5 Serve with fresh vegetable crudités, or with chunks of French bread or warm pitta breads.

VARIATION

If you come across smoked garlic, use it in this recipe – it tastes wonderful. There is no need to roast the smoked garlic, so omit the first step. This dip can also be used to baste vegetarian burgers.

Aïoli

This garlic mayonnaise features in many traditional Provençal recipes, but also makes a delicious dip, surrounded by a selection of vegetables.

NUTRITIONAL INFORMATION

Calories	239	Sugars	.........0g
Protein	.........1g	Fat	..........26g
Carbohydrate	....1g	Saturates	.......4g

15 mins — 0 mins

SERVES 6

INGREDIENTS

4 large garlic cloves, or to taste (see Cook's Tip, below)

2 large egg yolks

300 ml/10 fl oz extra-virgin olive oil

1–2 tbsp lemon juice

1 tbsp fresh white breadcrumbs

sea salt and pepper

TO SERVE

a selection of raw vegetables, such as sliced red peppers, courgette slices, whole spring onions and tomato wedges

a selection of blanched and cooled vegetables, such as baby artichoke hearts, cauliflower or broccoli florets, or French beans

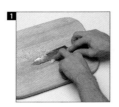  

COOK'S TIP

The amount of garlic in a traditional Provençal aïoli is a matter of personal taste. Local cooks use 2 cloves per person as a rule of thumb, but this version is slightly milder, although still bursting with flavour.

1 Finely chop the garlic on a chopping board. Add a pinch of sea salt to the garlic and use the tip and broad side of a knife to work the garlic and salt into a smooth paste.

2 Transfer the garlic paste to a food processor. Add the egg yolks and process until well blended, scraping down the side of the bowl with a rubber spatula, if necessary.

3 With the motor running, slowly pour in the olive oil in a steady stream through the feeder tube, processing until a thick mayonnaise forms.

4 Add 1 tablespoon of the lemon juice and all the breadcrumbs and process again. Taste and add more lemon juice if necessary. Season to taste with sea salt and pepper.

5 Place the aïoli in a bowl, cover, and chill until ready to serve. To serve, place the bowl of aïoli on a large platter and surround with a selection of raw and lightly blanched vegetables.

Taramasalata with Pittas

Forget the artificially dyed, bright pink taramasalata sold in supermarkets. This is the version you will find in Greek homes.

NUTRITIONAL INFORMATION

Calories 279	Sugars 4g	
Protein 9g	Fat 21g	
Carbohydrate . . .14g	Saturates 3g	

🍞 20 mins   ⏱ 20 mins

SERVES 6

I N G R E D I E N T S

225 g/8 oz smoked cod's roe

1 small onion, finely chopped

1 garlic clove

55 g/2 oz fresh white bread (about 2 thick slices), crusts removed

finely grated rind of 1 lemon

about 4 tbsp lemon juice

150 ml/5 fl oz extra-virgin olive oil

6 tbsp hot water

salt and pepper

sprigs of fresh flat-leaved parsley, to garnish

T O   S E R V E

hollowed-out tomatoes

fresh salad leaves

P I T T A   W E D G E S

2 pitta breads

olive oil, for brushing

1 Remove the skin from the smoked cod's roe. Put the roe and onion in a food processor and process until well blended and smooth. Add the garlic and process again.

2 Break the bread into the food processor, then add the lemon rind and the lemon juice. Process again until the bread is well incorporated.

3 With the motor running, gradually add the olive oil through the feeder tube, as if making a mayonnaise. When all the oil is incorporated, add the hot water and process again. Add salt and pepper to taste, plus extra lemon juice if wished. Spoon into a bowl, cover with clingfilm, and chill until ready to serve.

4 To make the pitta wedges, use a serrated knife to cut the pittas in half horizontally through the centre. Cut each half into 6–8 wedges, depending on the size of the pittas. Place on a baking sheet and brush the inside surfaces of the wedges with olive oil.

5 Bake the wedges in a preheated oven, 180°C/350°F/Gas Mark 4, for 20 minutes. Place on wire racks to cool. Spoon the taramasalata into the tomato shells, garnish with parsley, and serve with pitta wedges for dipping and fresh salad leaves.

COOK'S TIP

If you see smoked grey mullet roe, buy it for this dish. It is more authentic – and finer tasting – than smoked cod's roe.

Sesame Breadsticks

The irregular shape of these Greek-style breadsticks adds to their appeal.
They are crisp and crunchy on the outside with a soft, chewy interior.

NUTRITIONAL INFORMATION		
Calories 61	Sugars 0g	
Protein 2g	Fat 2g	
Carbohydrate . . .10g	Saturates 0g	

1¾ hrs   15 mins

MAKES 32 STICKS

I N G R E D I E N T S

225 g/8 oz unbleached strong white flour,
plus extra for dusting

225 g/8 oz strong wholemeal flour

1 packet easy-blend dried yeast

2 tsp salt

½ tsp sugar

about 450 ml/16 fl oz lukewarm water

4 tbsp olive oil, plus extra for greasing

1 egg white, lightly beaten

sesame seeds, for sprinkling

1 Combine the flours, yeast, salt, and sugar in a bowl and make a well in the centre. Gradually stir in most of the water, and all the olive oil, to make a dough. Gradually add the remaining water, if necessary, drawing in all the flour.

2 Turn out on to a lightly floured work surface and knead the dough for about 10 minutes until smooth and elastic. Wash the bowl and lightly coat with olive oil.

3 Shape the dough into a ball, put it in the bowl, and turn it over so it is coated. Cover tightly with a tea towel or lightly oiled clingfilm and set aside in a warm place until the dough has doubled in volume. Meanwhile, line a baking sheet with baking paper.

4 Turn out the dough on to a lightly floured work surface and knead lightly. Divide the dough into 2 equal pieces. Roll each piece into a 40-cm/16-inch rope and then cut each rope into 8 equal pieces. Cut each piece in half again to make a total of 32 pieces.

5 Cover the dough you are not working with a tea towel or clingfilm to prevent it drying out. Roll each piece of dough into a thin 25-cm/10-inch rope on a very lightly floured work surface. Carefully transfer to the baking sheet.

6 Cover and set aside to rise for 10 minutes. Brush with egg white, then sprinkle evenly and thickly with sesame seeds. Bake in a preheated oven, 230°C/450°F/Gas Mark 8, for 10 minutes.

7 Brush again with egg white, and bake for another 5 minutes or until golden brown and crisp. Transfer the breadsticks to wire racks to cool.

Black Bean Nachos

This tasty black bean and cheese dip is packed with authentic Mexican flavours. It is fun to eat and will get any party off to a good start.

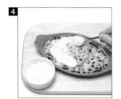

NUTRITIONAL INFORMATION

Calories	429	Sugars	.........2g
Protein	........28g	Fat	..........24g
Carbohydrate	...25g	Saturates	......15g

8¼ hrs   1¾ hrs

SERVES 4

I N G R E D I E N T S

225 g/8 oz dried black beans, or canned black beans, drained and rinsed

175–225 g/6–8 oz grated cheese, such as Cheddar, Asiago, fontina, pecorino, or a combination

about ¼ tsp cumin seeds or ground cumin

about 4 tbsp soured cream

TO GARNISH

pickled jalapeño chillies, thinly sliced (optional)

1 tbsp chopped fresh coriander

TO SERVE

handful of shredded lettuce

tortilla chips, to serve

1 If using dried black beans, use the following method. Place them in a bowl and cover with water. Soak overnight, then drain. Put in a saucepan, cover with water, and bring to the boil. Boil for 10 minutes, then lower the heat and simmer for about 1½ hours until tender. Drain well.

2 Spread the cooked or canned beans in the bottom of a shallow ovenproof dish, then sprinkle the cheese over the top. Sprinkle with cumin to taste.

3 Bake in a preheated oven, 190°C/ 375°F/Gas Mark 5, for 10–15 minutes or until the beans are cooked through and the cheese is bubbling and melted.

4 Remove the beans and cheese from the oven and spoon the soured cream on top. Add the jalapeño chillies, if using, and sprinkle over the coriander and lettuce.

5 Arrange the tortilla chips around the beans, sticking them into the mixture. Serve the nachos at once.

VARIATION
To add a meaty flavour, spoon chopped and browned chorizo on top of the beans, before sprinkling over the cheese, then cook as in step 3 – the combination is excellent. Finely chopped leftover cooked meat can also be added in this way.

Bite-sized Bhajis

Do not be surprised by the shapes these form – they are odd but look lovely when arranged on a tray with the yogurt dipping sauce.

NUTRITIONAL INFORMATION

Calories	122	Sugars	2g
Protein	2g	Fat	10g
Carbohydrate	6g	Saturates	1g

15 mins

15 mins

SERVES 20

I N G R E D I E N T S

2 heaped tbsp gram flour

½ tsp turmeric

½ tsp ground cumin seeds

1 tsp garam masala

pinch of cayenne pepper

1 egg

1 large onion, cut into quarters and sliced

1 tbsp chopped fresh coriander

3 tbsp breadcrumbs (optional)

vegetable oil, for deep-frying

salt

fresh coriander leaves, to garnish

S A U C E

1 tsp ground coriander seeds

1½ tsp ground cumin seeds

225 ml/8 fl oz natural yogurt

salt and pepper

COOK'S TIP

Make sure that the pan and all the utensils are properly dried before use. Do not let any water come into contact with the hot oil or the oil will spit and splutter, which could be dangerous.

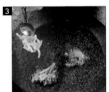

1 Put the gram flour into a large bowl and mix in the turmeric, cumin, garam masala and cayenne. Make a well in the centre and add the egg. Stir to form a sticky mixture. Add the onion and sprinkle in a little salt. Add the coriander and stir. If the mixture is not stiff enough, stir in the breadcrumbs.

2 Heat the oil for deep-frying over a medium heat until fairly hot – it should just be starting to smoke.

3 Push teaspoonfuls of the mixture into the oil with a second teaspoon to form fairly round balls. The bhajis should firm up quite quickly. Cook in batches of 8–10, stirring so that they brown evenly. Drain on kitchen paper and keep them warm in the oven until ready to serve.

4 To make the sauce, roast the spices in a frying pan. Remove from the heat and stir in the yogurt. Season well.

Samosas

Samosas, which are a kind of Indian pasty, make excellent party snacks. In India, they are popular snacks at roadside stands.

NUTRITIONAL INFORMATION

Calories 261	Sugars 0.4g
Protein 2g	Fat 23g
Carbohydrate . . .13g	Saturates 4g

🌀 🌀 🌀

🍲 40 mins ⏱ 40 mins

SERVES 12

I N G R E D I E N T S

P A S T R Y

100 g/3½ oz self-raising flour

½ tsp salt

3 tbsp butter, cut into small pieces

4 tbsp water

F I L L I N G

3 medium potatoes, boiled

1 tsp finely chopped root ginger

1 tsp crushed garlic

½ tsp white cumin seeds

½ tsp mustard seeds

1 tsp salt

½ tsp crushed red chillies

2 tbsp lemon juice

2 small green chillies, finely chopped

ghee or oil, for deep-frying

1 Sift the flour and salt into a bowl. Add the pieces of butter and then rub into the flour until the mixture resembles fine breadcrumbs.

2 Pour in the water and mix with a fork to form a dough. Pat it into a ball and knead for 5 minutes or until smooth. Cover and leave to rise.

3 To make the filling, mash the boiled potatoes gently and mix with the ginger, garlic, white cumin seeds, mustard seeds, salt, crushed red chillies, lemon juice and green chillies.

4 Break small balls off the dough and roll each out very thinly to form a round. Cut in half, dampen the edges, and shape into cones. Fill the cones with a little of the filling, dampen the top and bottom edges of the cones, and pinch together to seal. Set aside.

5 Fill a deep pan one-third full with ghee or oil and heat to 180°C/350°F, or until a small cube of bread browns in 30 seconds. Carefully lower the samosas into the oil, a few at a time, and cook for 2–3 minutes or until golden brown. Remove from the oil and drain thoroughly on kitchen paper. Serve hot or cold.

Toasted Nibbles

These tiny cheese balls are rolled in fresh herbs, toasted nuts, or paprika to make tasty nibbles for parties, buffets or pre-dinner drinks.

NUTRITIONAL INFORMATION

Calories . . . . .310 Sugars 1g
Protein . . . . .15g Fat 27g
Carbohydrate . . . .1g Saturates 12g

40 mins   5 mins

SERVES 4

I N G R E D I E N T S

115 g/4 oz ricotta cheese

115 g/4 oz Double Gloucester or Cheddar cheese, finely grated

2 tsp chopped fresh parsley

55 g/2 oz chopped mixed nuts

3 tbsp chopped fresh mixed herbs, such as parsley, chives, marjoram, lovage, and chervil

2 tbsp mild paprika

pepper

sprigs of fresh herbs, to garnish

1 Combine the ricotta with the Double Gloucester or Cheddar cheese. Add the parsley, season with pepper, and mix together until thoroughly combined.

2 Form the mixture into small balls and place on a plate. Cover and chill in the refrigerator for about 20 minutes until they are firm.

3 Sprinkle the chopped nuts on to a baking sheet and place them under a preheated grill until lightly browned. Take care because they can easily burn. Remove from the grill and set aside to cool.

4 Place the nuts, mixed herbs and paprika into 3 separate small bowls. Remove the cheese balls from the refrigerator and divide into 3 equal piles. Roll 1 quantity of the cheese balls in the nuts, 1 quantity in the herbs, and 1 quantity in the paprika.

5 Arrange the coated cheese balls alternately on a large serving platter. Cover and chill in the refrigerator until ready to serve, and then garnish with sprigs of fresh herbs.

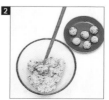

Spicy Prawn Wedges

This recipe is a winning combination of textures and flavours – spiced prawns and creamy avocado – served on crisply cooked tortilla wedges.

NUTRITIONAL INFORMATION

Calories	255	Sugars	.........2g
Protein	........15g	Fat	..........13g
Carbohydrate	...22g	Saturates	.......4g

4¼ hrs   12–15 mins

SERVES 8–10

I N G R E D I E N T S

500 g/1 lb 2 oz cooked prawns

4 garlic cloves, finely chopped

½ tsp mild chilli powder

½ tsp ground cumin

juice of 1 lime

1 ripe tomato, diced

6 corn tortillas

vegetable oil, for cooking

2 avocados

200 ml/7 fl oz soured cream

salt

mild chilli powder, to garnish

wedges of lime, to serve

1 Place the prawns in a bowl with the garlic, chilli powder, cumin, lime juice and tomato. Add salt to taste and stir gently to mix. Chill for at least 4 hours, or overnight to let the flavours mingle.

2 Cut the tortillas into wedges. Heat a little oil in a non-stick frying pan, add a batch of tortilla wedges, and cook over a medium heat until crisp. Repeat with the remaining wedges and transfer to a serving platter.

3 Cut each avocado in half around the stone. Twist the halves apart in opposite directions, then remove the stone with a knife. Carefully peel off the skin and dice the flesh. Gently stir the avocado flesh into the prawn mixture.

4 Top each tortilla wedge with a small mound of the prawn and avocado mixture. Finish with a dab of soured cream, garnish with a light sprinkling of chilli powder, and serve immediately with wedges of lime.

COOK'S TIP

For speed, you can use crisp corn tortillas or nacho chips (not too salty) instead of the corn tortillas.

Feta Cheese Tartlets

These crisp-baked bread cases, filled with sliced tomatoes, feta cheese, black olives and quail's eggs, are quick to make and taste delicious.

NUTRITIONAL INFORMATION

Calories 570	Sugars 3g	
Protein 14g	Fat 42g	
Carbohydrate . . .36g	Saturates 23g	

 30 mins   10 mins

SERVES 4

INGREDIENTS

8 slices bread from a medium-cut large loaf

125 g/4½ oz butter, melted

125 g/4½ oz feta cheese, cut into small cubes

4 cherry tomatoes, cut into wedges

8 black or green olives, stoned and halved

8 quail's eggs, hard-boiled

sprigs of fresh parsley, to garnish

DRESSING

2 tbsp olive oil

1 tbsp wine vinegar

1 tsp whole-grain mustard

pinch of caster sugar

salt and pepper

1 Remove the crusts from the bread. Trim the bread into squares and flatten each piece with a rolling pin.

2 Brush the bread squares with melted butter, and then arrange them in bun or muffin tins. Press a piece of crumpled foil into each bread shell to secure in place. Bake the shells in a preheated oven, 190°C/375°F/Gas Mark 5, for 10 minutes or until crisp and browned.

3 Meanwhile, mix together the feta cheese, tomatoes and olives. Shell the eggs and cut them into quarters. To make the dressing, mix together the olive oil, vinegar, mustard and sugar. Season to taste.

4 Remove the bread shells from the oven and discard the foil. Leave to cool.

5 Just before serving, fill the bread shells with the cheese and tomato mixture. Arrange the eggs on top and spoon over the dressing. Garnish with sprigs of fresh parsley.

Crostini alla Fiorentina

Serve your guests this delicious treat spread on small slices of crusty toasted bread. It is also ideal as an appetizer with drinks.

NUTRITIONAL INFORMATION

Calories	 393	Sugars	.... 2g
Protein	.... 17g	Fat	.... 25g
Carbohydrate	... 19g	Saturates	.... 9g

10 mins

40–45 mins

SERVES 4

INGREDIENTS

3 tbsp olive oil

1 onion, chopped

1 celery stick, chopped

1 carrot, chopped

1–2 garlic cloves, crushed

125 g/4½ oz chicken livers

125 g/4½ oz calf's, lamb's or pig's liver

150 ml/5 fl oz red wine

1 tbsp tomato purée

2 tbsp chopped fresh parsley

3–4 canned anchovy fillets, finely chopped

2 tbsp stock or water

2–3 tbsp butter

1 tbsp capers

salt and pepper

chopped fresh parsley, to garnish

small slices of crusty bread, toasted, to serve

1 Heat the oil in a pan, add the onion, celery, carrot and garlic, and cook gently for 4–5 minutes or until the onion is soft but not coloured.

2 Meanwhile, rinse and dry the chicken livers. Dry the calf's liver or other liver, and slice into strips. Add all the liver to the pan and cook gently for a few minutes until the strips are well sealed on all sides.

3 Add half of the wine and cook until it has mostly evaporated. Then add the rest of the wine, with the tomato purée, half of the parsley, the anchovy fillets, the stock or water, a little salt and plenty of black pepper.

4 Cover the pan and leave to simmer, stirring occasionally, for 15–20 minutes or until tender and most of the liquid has been absorbed.

5 Let the mixture cool a little, then either coarsely grind or put into a food processor and process to a chunky purée.

6 Return to the pan and add the butter, capers, and remaining parsley. Heat through gently until the butter melts. Adjust the seasoning and turn out into a bowl. Serve warm or cold spread on the slices of crusty bread and sprinkled with chopped parsley.

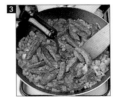

Mozzarella Snack

These deep-fried mozzarella sandwiches make a tasty party snack. Alternatively, smaller triangles can be served with drinks.

NUTRITIONAL INFORMATION

Calories ....379 Sugars 4g
Protein ....20g Fat 22g
Carbohydrate ...28g Saturates 5g

🍳 20 mins   🕐 5–10 mins

SERVES 4

I N G R E D I E N T S

8 slices bread, preferably slightly stale, crusts removed

100 g/3½ oz mozzarella cheese, thickly sliced

50 g/1¾ oz black olives, chopped

8 canned anchovy fillets, drained and chopped

16 fresh basil leaves

4 eggs, beaten

150 ml/5 fl oz milk

oil, for deep-frying

salt and pepper

sprigs of fresh basil, to garnish

1 Using a sharp knife, cut each slice of bread into 2 triangles. Top 8 of the bread triangles with the mozzarella slices, olives and chopped anchovies.

2 Place the basil leaves on top and season with salt and pepper to taste.

3 Lay the other 8 triangles of bread over the top and press down round the edges to seal.

4 Mix together the eggs and milk and pour into an ovenproof dish. Add the sandwiches and let them soak for about 5 minutes.

5 Heat the oil in a large pan to 180–190°C/350–375°F, or until a cube of bread browns in 30 seconds.

6 Before cooking the sandwiches, squeeze the edges together again.

7 Carefully place the sandwiches in the oil and deep-fry, turning once, for 2 minutes or until golden. Remove the sandwiches with a slotted spoon and drain them on absorbent kitchen paper. Garnish with sprigs of fresh basil and serve immediately.

Masa Tartlets

These little golden tartlets are packed with Mexican flavours and make a colourful addition to party fare.

NUTRITIONAL INFORMATION

Calories	474	Sugars	.........4g
Protein	........11g	Fat	..........23g
Carbohydrate	...58g	Saturates	.......8g

35 mins   30 mins

SERVES 4

I N G R E D I E N T S

PASTRY

8–10 tbsp masa harina

3 tbsp plain flour

pinch of baking powder

about 225 ml/8 fl oz warm water

vegetable oil, for cooking

FILLING

375 g/13 oz pinto beans or refried beans, heated through

1 avocado, stoned, sliced, and tossed with lime juice

85 g/3 oz queso fresco, fresh cream cheese, or crumbled feta

salsa of your choice

2 spring onions, thinly sliced

TO GARNISH

sprigs of fresh flat-leaved parsley

lemon wedges

1 To make the pastry, mix the masa harina with the plain flour and baking powder in a bowl, then mix in enough warm water to make a firm yet moist dough.

2 Pinch off about a walnut-sized piece of dough and, using your fingers, shape it into a tiny tartlet shape, pressing and pinching to make it as thin as possible without falling apart. Repeat with the remaining dough.

3 Heat a layer of oil in a deep frying pan until it is smoking. Add a batch of tartlets to the hot oil and cook, spooning the hot fat into the centre of the tartlets and turning once, until golden on all sides.

4 Using a slotted spoon, remove the tartlets from the hot oil and drain on kitchen paper. Place on a baking sheet and keep warm in the oven on a low temperature while cooking the remaining tartlets.

5 To serve, fill each pastry case with the warmed beans, avocado, cheese, salsa, and spring onions. Garnish with sprigs of parsley and lemon wedges and serve immediately.

Mini Pizzas

These tiny pizzas are known in Italy as *pizette*. This quantity will make 8 individual pizzas, or 16 cocktail pizzas to go with drinks.

NUTRITIONAL INFORMATION

Calories ....139 Sugars 1g
Protein ....4g Fat 6g
Carbohydrate ...18g Saturates 1g

🍞 🍞 🍞

🥔 1¼ hrs   🕐 15 mins

SERVES 8

I N G R E D I E N T S

B A S I C   P I Z Z A   D O U G H

2 tsp dried yeast

1 tsp sugar

about 225 ml/8 fl oz warm water

350 g/12 oz strong plain flour, plus extra
    for dusting

1 tsp salt

1 tbsp olive oil, plus extra for greasing

T O P P I N G

2 courgettes

100 ml/3½ fl oz passata

75 g/2¾ oz pancetta, diced

50 g/1¾ oz stoned black olives, chopped

1 tbsp mixed dried herbs

2 tbsp olive oil

salt and pepper

1 Place the yeast and sugar in a jug and mix with 4 tablespoons of the water. Set the yeast mixture aside in a warm place for 15 minutes or until frothy.

2 Mix the flour with the salt and make a well in the centre. Add the oil, the yeast mixture, and the remaining water. Using a wooden spoon, mix together to form a smooth dough.

3 Turn the dough out on to a floured work surface; knead for 4–5 minutes or until smooth. Return the dough to the bowl, cover with an oiled sheet of clingfilm, and leave to rise for 30 minutes or until the dough has doubled in size.

4 Knead the dough for 2 minutes and divide it into 8 balls (or 16 balls for cocktail pizzas). Roll out each portion thinly to form circles, then carefully transfer them to an oiled baking sheet, pushing out the edges until even. The dough should be no more than 5 mm/¼ inch thick because it will rise during cooking.

5 To make the topping, finely grate the courgettes. Cover with kitchen paper and leave to stand for 10 minutes to absorb some of the juices.

6 Spread the passata over the pizza bases and top each one with the grated courgettes, and the pancetta and olives. Season with pepper, add mixed dried herbs to taste, and drizzle with oil.

7 Bake in a preheated oven, 200°C/ 400°F/Gas Mark 6, for 15 minutes or until crispy. Season with salt and pepper to taste and serve hot.

Fresh Tomato Tarts

These tomato-flavoured tarts should be eaten as fresh as possible to enjoy the flaky and crisp buttery puff pastry.

NUTRITIONAL INFORMATION

Calories . . . . .217 Sugars 3g
Protein . . . . .5g Fat 14g
Carbohydrate . . .18g Saturates 1g

35 mins   20 mins

SERVES 6

I N G R E D I E N T S

1–2 tbsp plain flour, for dusting

250 g/9 oz ready-made puff pastry dough, thawed if frozen

1 egg, beaten

2 tbsp pesto sauce (available from many shops and delicatessens)

6 plum tomatoes, sliced

salt and pepper

fresh thyme leaves, to garnish (optional)

1 On a lightly floured work surface, roll out the dough to a rectangle measuring 30 x 25 cm/12 x 10 inches.

2 Cut the rectangle in half lengthways, then divide each half into 3 pieces to make 6 even-sized rectangles. Chill in the refrigerator for 20 minutes.

3 Lightly score the edges of the dough rectangles and then brush with the beaten egg.

4 Spread the pesto over the rectangles, dividing it equally among them, leaving a 2.5-cm/1-inch border around each one.

5 Arrange the tomato slices along the centre of each rectangle on top of the pesto.

6 Season well with salt and pepper to taste and lightly sprinkle with fresh thyme leaves, if using.

7 Bake the tarts in a preheated oven, 200°C/400°F/Gas Mark 6, for about 15–20 minutes until they are well risen and golden brown.

8 Transfer the tarts to warm serving plates and serve while they are still piping hot and crisp.

VARIATION

Instead of individual tarts, roll the dough out to form 1 large rectangle. Spoon over the pesto and arrange the tomatoes over the top.

Mini Cheese & Onion Tarts

Serve these delicious little savoury tarts as irresistible finger food at buffets or drinks parties, or take them on a picnic.

NUTRITIONAL INFORMATION

Calories	114	Sugars	.........1g
Protein	.........3g	Fat	...........9g
Carbohydrate	....7g	Saturates	.......5g

 45 mins   25 mins

SERVES 12

I N G R E D I E N T S

P A S T R Y

100 g/3½ oz plain flour, plus extra
  for dusting

¼ tsp salt

6 tbsp butter, cut into small pieces

1–2 tbsp water

F I L L I N G

1 egg, beaten

100 ml/3½ fl oz single cream

50 g/1¾ oz Red Leicester or Cheddar
  cheese, grated

3 spring onions, finely chopped

salt

cayenne pepper

1 To make the dough, sift the flour and salt into a mixing bowl. Add the butter and rub it in with your fingertips until the

mixture resembles breadcrumbs. Stir in the water and mix to form a dough. Form into a ball, cover, and refrigerate for 30 minutes.

2 Roll out the dough on a lightly floured work surface. Using a 7.5-cm/3-inch biscuit cutter, stamp out 12 circles from the dough and line a shallow muffin tin.

3 To make the filling, whisk together the beaten egg, single cream, grated

cheese and chopped spring onions in a jug. Season to taste with salt and cayenne.

4 Pour the filling mixture into the pastry cases and bake in a preheated oven, 180°C/350°F/Gas Mark 4, for about 20–25 minutes or until the filling is just set.

5 Serve at once, if serving warm, or transfer to a wire rack to cool.

COOK'S TIP

If you use 175 g/6 oz of ready-made pastry instead of making it yourself, these tarts can be made in minutes.

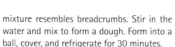

Roman Focaccia

Roman focaccia makes a delicious party snack, or a quick and tasty supper when served with a selection of cheeses and salad.

NUTRITIONAL INFORMATION

Calories	119	Sugars	.........2g
Protein	.........3g	Fat	...........2g
Carbohydrate	...24g	Saturates	.....0.3g

1 hr · 45 mins

MAKES 16 SQUARES

INGREDIENTS

2 tsp dried yeast

1 tsp granulated sugar

300 ml/10 fl oz lukewarm water

450 g/1 lb strong white flour

2 tsp salt

3 tbsp chopped fresh rosemary

2 tbsp olive oil, plus extra for greasing

450 g/1 lb mixed red and white onions, sliced into rings

4 garlic cloves, sliced

1 Place the yeast and the sugar in a bowl and mix with 100 ml/3½ fl oz of the water. Let the mixture ferment in a warm place for 15 minutes.

2 Sift the flour with the salt into a large bowl. Add the yeast mixture, half of the rosemary, and the remaining water, and mix to form a smooth dough. Knead the dough for 4 minutes.

3 Cover the dough with oiled clingfilm and leave to rise for 30 minutes or until doubled in size.

4 Meanwhile, heat the remaining oil in a large pan. Add the onions and garlic and cook over a low heat for 5 minutes or until soft. Cover the pan and continue to cook for another 7–8 minutes or until the onions are lightly caramelised.

5 Knead the dough for 1–2 minutes, then roll out to a square. It should be no more than 5 mm/¼ inch thick because it will rise during cooking. Place the dough on a large baking sheet, pushing out the edges until even.

6 Spread the onions evenly over the dough, then sprinkle the surface with the remaining rosemary.

7 Bake in a preheated oven, 200°C/400°F/Gas Mark 6, for 25–30 minutes or until a golden brown colour. Cut the focaccia into 16 squares and serve immediately while it is still warm.

Provençal Tart

This tart is full of colour and flavour from the courgettes and red and green peppers. It makes a great change from a quiche Lorraine.

NUTRITIONAL INFORMATION

Calories 355	Sugars 5g
Protein 5g	Fat 29g
Carbohydrate ...21g	Saturates 9g

10–15 mins   55 mins

SERVES 6

INGREDIENTS

PASTRY

250 g/9 oz ready-made puff pastry, thawed if frozen

1–2 tbsp plain flour, for dusting

FILLING

3 tbsp olive oil

2 red peppers, deseeded and diced

2 green peppers, deseeded and diced

150 ml/5 fl oz double cream

1 egg

2 courgettes, sliced

salt and pepper

1 To make the pastry, roll out the dough on a lightly floured work surface and use it to line a 20-cm/8-inch loose-bottomed flan tin. Chill in the refrigerator for 20 minutes.

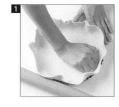

2 Meanwhile, to make the filling, heat 2 tablespoons of the oil in a pan. Add the peppers and cook over a low heat, stirring, for 8 minutes until softened.

3 Whisk the cream and egg together in a bowl, season, and stir in the peppers.

4 Heat the remaining olive oil in a pan and cook the courgette slices for 4–5 minutes until lightly browned.

5 Pour the egg and bell pepper mixture into the pastry case.

6 Arrange the courgette slices around the edge of the tart.

7 Bake in a preheated oven, 180°C/350°F/Gas Mark 4, for 35–40 minutes or until just set and golden brown. Serve at once or leave to cool and serve cold.

COOK'S TIP

This recipe could be used to make 6 individual tarts – use 15 x 10-cm/6 x 4-inch tins and bake for 20 minutes.